HAIL!
ANCIENT EGYPTIANS

Jen Green

WAYLAND

WAYLAND

This edition published in 2012 by Wayland

Copyright © 2011 Brown Bear Books Ltd.

Wayland
Hachette Children's Books
338 Euston Road
London NW1 3BH

Wayland Australia
Level 17/207 Kent Street
Sydney, NSW 2000

Brown Bear Books Ltd.
First Floor
9–17 St. Albans Place
London
N1 0NX

Author: Jen Green
Managing editor: Miranda Smith
Designer: Lorna Phillips
Picture researcher: Clare Newman
Design manager: David Poole
Editorial director: Lindsey Lowe
Children's publisher: Anne O'Daly
Consultant: Dr Paul G. Bahn

British Library Cataloguing in Publication Data

Green, Jen.
    Ancient Egyptians. — (Hail!)
    1. Egypt—History—To 322 B.C.—Juvenile literature.
    2. Egypt—Civilization—To 322 B.C.—Juvenile literature.
    I. Title II. Series
    932'.01-dc23

ISBN–13: 978 0 7502 6747 2

Printed in China

Wayland is a division of Hachette Children's Books, an
Hachette UK company.
www.hachette.co.uk

Websites

The website addresses (URLs) included in this book were valid at the time of going to press. However, because of the nature of the internet, it is possible that some addresses may have changed, or sites may have changed or closed down since publication. While the author and publisher regret any inconvenience this may cause the readers, no responsibility for any such changes can be accepted by either the author or the publisher.

PICTURE ACKNOWLEDGEMENTS
Key: b = bottom, bgr = background, c = centre, is = insert , l = left, mtg = montage, r = right, t = top.

Front Cover: Shutterstock: Photo Sani tr; Thinkstock: l, br; Topham: The Granger Collection cr.
Interior: Alamy: Ancient Art & Architecture Collection 18cr, Ancient Nile 21cl, Bygone Times 20tl, Interfoto 24l; Bridgeman Art Library: 13cl; Corbis: Brooklyn Museum 22bl, Poodles Rock 8cl, Robert Harding World Imagery 26c, The Art Archive 17clb, Sandro Vannini 15bl, 18cl, 19bl, 21trr, Werner Forman 14br, 15tl, Yann Arthus-Bertrand 10br, Roger Wood 17c; iStockphoto: Brytta 16cr, Melissa Carroll 17tcl, Dgmata 17clt, Jose Ignacia Soto 23tl, Eric Jamison 14bl, David Kerkhoff 24ct, 25cr, Pavel Konovalov 27bc, Andrei Mastio 16bl, Nico Olay 11cr, Dra Schwartz 14c, Els Van Der Gun 22tr; Jupiter Images: 5bc, 25tc, 16br; Mary Evans Picture Library: 6bl, 19c; Shutterstock: Andesign101 9bl, Architecte 8bc, Carlos Arquelles 29br, Kitch Bain 28blb, Vorm in Beeld 14tl, Goran Bogicevic 21tll, Kate Bross 4cr, Katrina Brown 27trb, 27br, Buniiholls 25cl, C J Photo 24brt, CLM 18/19 bgr, Jose Gil 12bl, Tatiana Grozetskaya 21tlr, Ramzi Hachicho 5bl, 11bl, 23b, Lim Yong Hian 10l, Jose Ignacio Soto 9cr, 19tl, Innocent 15bct, Eric Isselee 13br, 15brt, 28bc, Karkas 16tc, 17tcr, Kletr 28blt, Biaz Kure 10tr, Loop All 14crl, Georgy Markov 15bcb, Max Stock Photo 30/31, Artem Mazunov 25brb, William Milner 29bl, Moeadv 27tr, Palto 6tr, Pannev 28tl, Kirsty Pargeter 24tr, 24cb, 24brb, 25brt, Thomas M. Perkins 15cl, Photo Sani 20tr, Rodho 11tl, Scott Rothstein 20/21, Olga Rotko 17br, Klena Schweitzer 21trl, Sculpies 9tr, Kristian Sekulic 28bct, Sergieiev 14bcl, Maksymillian Skolik 14bcr, Steffan Foerster Photography 29tc, Sufi 14crr, Ian Tragen 29tr, Tsr 15brb, Valentyn Volkov 28tr, VP Design 14cl, Vladimir Wrangel 16cl, 21tcr, Konstantin Yolshin 7br, M. Yotis 12/13 bgr, Olga Zaichenko 14bcr, 15cr; Still Pictures: Biosphoto 28c; Thinkstock: 3tr, 3bc, 9cl, 10c, 13bc, 17cr, 18br, 26bl; Topham: 27cl, 29cr, RIA Novosti 7c, Stepleton/HIP 12tr, The Granger Collection 7tr, Charles Walker 18tr, The British Library/HIP 23tr; Werner Forman: Egyptian Museum, Cairo 26br, E. Strouhal 5br, 21cr; Wikimedia: 6br.

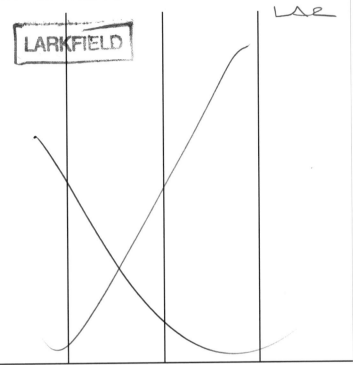

CONTENTS

ANCIENT EGYPT

Welcome to the fabulous world of ancient Egypt. Around 3300 BCE our ancestors, who were farmers, founded one of the world's first great civilisations on the banks of the River Nile. Egyptian pharaohs, tombs and gods are all world-famous. *HAIL!* reviews our finest achievements so that you can decide for yourself just what makes ancient Egypt great.

SECRET OF SUCCESS

The key to our success is simple — dirt and water! The River Nile keeps us alive and helps our great civilisation flourish.

Every year the river floods, covering the narrow strip of land along the bank with rich, dark silt. This black dirt allows us to produce all the food we need — and more. We sell the extra, which has made us fabulously wealthy. So thanks, O mighty river, and all hail, black dirt!

HAIL! QUIZ WHY IS EGYPT FAMOUS?

Take part in our readers' quiz to select the key sources of Egypt's fame.

1. PHARAOHS
Since about 1500 BCE, our kings have been called pharaohs — this title means "Great House". The pharaoh rules all of Egypt. He is chief priest and army commander. The throne passes from father to son, forming a royal line that is called a dynasty.

2. PYRAMIDS
Egyptians are famous all over the world for our magnificent tombs and temples. None are more amazing than the pyramids, which were built as tombs for the pharaohs. The great pyramids of Giza are top tourist attractions, even in ancient times.

3. MUMMIES
We are firm believers in life after death. We preserve the bodies of our dead for the afterlife through the process of mummification. Some of our mummies will still be in good shape 4,000 years from now!

4. GODS AND GODDESSES
Egyptians are a religious lot. We worship hundreds of different gods and goddesses in our shrines and temples. To prevent confusion, we draw, paint and sculpt many of our holy ones with an animal's head. This records their star quality for posterity.

5. WRITING
Around 3300 BCE, we invented one of the world's oldest scripts. Hieroglyphics are a form of picture writing. With more than 700 symbols, our script is fiendishly complicated, and scholars called scribes are pretty much the only ones who can read it. (Most of us can't read to save our lives!)

Submit Your Answer

SEE INSIDE:

Makeover Mummy pp. 20-21

Grand Designs pp. 10-11

Style File pp. 16-17

REGULAR CONTRIBUTORS: Cleopatra, Nefertiti, Wise Man Hesire, Tutankhamun

WHAT'S ON TV?

Egyptians are proud of their amazing past and glorious present. Three thousand years of history are divided into the Old, Middle and New Kingdoms. The Early Dynastic Era came before that, and the Late Period came after, with a couple of Intermediate Periods in between. As part of history week our national network, Pharaoh TV, presents five nights of programmes celebrating our wondrous past.

MONDAY

EARLY DYNASTIC NIGHT

A night of programmes celebrating the first great era of Egyptian history (3100–2685 BCE).

7:00 p.m. HOW IT ALL BEGAN
In 3100 BCE, King Narmer united Upper and Lower Egypt to form the world's first nation state. An account of his victories and coronation with the double crown representing the unified Egypt.

8:00 p.m. MEET THE ANCESTOR: Narmer the Nasty
A profile of the great king (left) — known for his habit of leading his enemies by a rope threaded through the nose. Was Narmer really nasty?

9:00 p.m. DIE-NASTY
Latest episode in the long-running soap opera set in the royal palace. The pharaoh takes a new wife. The queen is not amused.

TUESDAY

OLD KINGDOM NIGHT

Tonight's focus is on an era of strong rule and the great age of pyramid building (2685–2180 BCE).

7:00 p.m. PYRAMID-MANIA
We investigate the fad of pyramid building in Old Kingdom times.

8:15 p.m. MEET THE ANCESTOR: King Khufu
A look at the pharaoh who built the largest pyramid. Reports say Khufu (right) once had a man's head chopped off just to see if his magician could fix it back on again, but is this story true?

9:00 p.m. DIE-NASTY
The queen falls for a very handsome young scribe.
10:00 p.m. CHANGING TOMBS
Our team of expert craftsmen have just 24 hours to redecorate your tomb.

WEDNESDAY

MIDDLE KINGDOM NIGHT

Tonight the Middle Kingdom (2055–1650 BCE) is in the spotlight. During this era, powerful kings ruled from the city of Thebes.

7:00 p.m. WHAT'S IN A NAME?
Middle Kingdom rulers include kings Amenemhat I–IV, Senusret I–III and Sobekneferu. What on earth possessed the pharaohs to choose such unpronounceable names?

8:00 p.m. PYRAMID MAZE
In 2055 BCE, Amenemhat III (right) built a maze inside his pyramid to foil tomb robbers. In this popular game show, teams of thieves compete to penetrate the maze and steal the treasure.

9:00 p.m. DIE-NASTY
The pharaoh arranges a horrible death for the young scribe.

THURSDAY

NEW KINGDOM NIGHT

Some of our most famous pharaohs ruled in this era (1550–1069 BCE) — the warrior Ramesses II, boy-king Tutankhamun and one of our female rulers, Hatshepsut.

7:00 p.m. AKHENATEN — ODD ONE OUT
A profile of the oddball pharaoh (above) who temporarily transformed Egypt's religion by enforcing worship of only one god, the Sun god Aten.

8:15 p.m. YES, YOUR MAJESTY
Comedy series based on the life of Queen Hatshepsut, who ruled as a male pharaoh.

9:00 p.m. DIE-NASTY
The queen arranges a horrible death for the pharaoh. Her teenage stepson is crowned.

10:00 p.m. MEET THE ANCESTOR — RAMESSES II
Great warrior, great builder — and great liar?

FRIDAY LATE NIGHT ERA

During this era (1069–30 BCE) Egypt was ruled by a series of foreign empires. In 332 BCE, the Greek general Alexander conquered Egypt, establishing the Ptolemy dynasty. Finally Rome took over in 30 BCE.

7:00 p.m. WHAT THE PERSIANS DID
A look at Egypt under Persian rule.

9:00 p.m. DIE-NASTY
The teenage pharaoh arranges a horrible death for his stepmother…

10:00 p.m. WHAT THE ROMANS DID
Similar to the Persians, but different masters.

8:15 p.m. CLEO — QUEEN OR COURTESAN?
Cleopatra was the last of the Ptolemies and the last pharaoh. Her many lovers included Roman generals Julius Caesar and Mark Antony. We delve into the love life of our most famous queen.

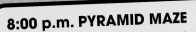

GLOBE TROTTERS'

GUIDE TO EGYPT

Ancient Egypt is the world's longest, thinnest country. Civilisation only extends a few kilometres on either side of the River Nile, which runs the length of the country. Beyond that is dusty desert. Join our travel team as they cruise along the Nile, rating the top sights of our fair land.

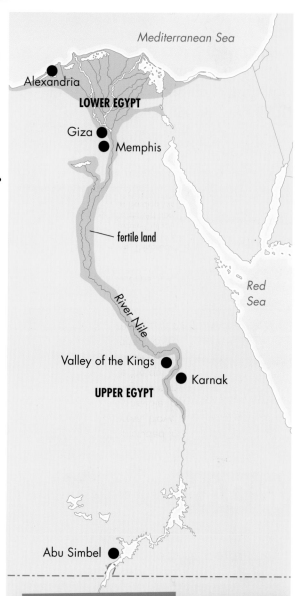

Mediterranean Sea

Alexandria

LOWER EGYPT

Giza

Memphis

fertile land

Red Sea

River Nile

Valley of the Kings

Karnak

UPPER EGYPT

Abu Simbel

ALEXANDRIA

The capital city under the Ptolemies. Founded by Alexander the Great in 332 BCE. A centre for learning with the world's biggest library.
Rating: *Top sights include the Pharos (left), the world's first lighthouse, which was built in 270 BCE.*

KARNAK

The Great Temple of Amun-Re has the world's largest columned hall, with over 130 columns soaring 20 metres (66 feet) up in the air.
Rating: *Fantastic, but take care not to twist your neck.*

NILE DELTA

The large, swampy delta where the River Nile meets the sea is Egypt's main farming region. We call this area Lower Egypt. The land either side of the river higher up is called Upper Egypt.
Rating: *Lush and green, but mosquitoes can be a problem.*

OUR BOATMAN POINTS OUT THE SIGHTS:

"See those workmen cutting papyrus reeds? We use papyrus to make boats, sandals, ropes and paper. You can see all kinds of craft on the river — fishing skiffs, grain barges and pleasure boats. Watch out for floating logs — they may be crocodiles."

GIZA

Location of *the* pyramids — Egypt's top attraction. The Sphinx is another must-see — a giant statue of a creature with a pharaoh's head and lion's body.
Rating: *This is Egypt's top tourist attraction, but beware of tomb robbers around the place.*

VALLEY OF THE KINGS

The burial place of Middle and New Kingdom pharaohs close to their capital, Thebes.
Rating: *The tombs are dug into the hillside. The nearby workmen's village of Deir el-Medina is worth a visit to soak up the local atmosphere and culture.*

MEMPHIS

Egypt's capital in Old Kingdom times. The Giza pyramids are a short donkey ride away. The first pyramid ever built is in the Saqqara necropolis close by.
Rating: *Lots to see. Don't miss the temples of Ptah and Apis, and the two statues of Ramesses II.*

ABU SIMBEL

This temple, built by Ramesses II, is a whopper. Guarded by four giant statues of the king and decorated with scenes of his greatest battles.
Rating: *Ramesses II was a bighead, but his temple is awesome.*

GRAND DESIGNS

The latest must-have architectural ideas

PYRAMIDS
WHAT'S THE POINT?

The point of a pyramid is to bury the king in style. The tiny burial chamber at its heart holds the king's body — and the fabulous treasure he will need in the afterlife. Of course, the actual point of the pyramid is very high — 146 metres (479 ft) in the case of the Great Pyramid of Giza (below).

Stairway to Heaven

The very first pyramid was built around 2650 BCE. It was designed by the architect Imhotep as a burial place for his boss, King Djoser.

Imhotep says: "I started with a rectangular tomb called a mastaba. Then I thought, why not build a series of mastabas, one on top of the other? The result was a step pyramid — like a stairway for the king's soul to rise to heaven."

WHAT WENT WRONG?

The wonky tiers of the Meidum Pyramid rise from a huge pile of rubble. This pyramid had weak foundations and collapsed soon after completion. Ah well, you can't win them all. Back to the drawing board — and no doubt, "Off with his head" in the case of the architect.

STATE OF THE ART

Around 2600 BCE, King Sneferu built the first pyramid with smooth sides. Faced with the finest limestone, the smooth shape gleamed in the sunlight. Everyone thought the new design was so cool it was followed ever afterwards, and step pyramids became ancient history.

The pyramids of Egypt are the wonder of the ancient world. Not all of the grand designs of the pyramids worked out as planned. *HAIL!*'s expert reviews the very finest Egyptian architecture — and the structures that went wrong.

GRAND OPENING!

2589 BCE. The largest pyramid of all time has just been completed at Giza. Built for King Khufu, it is made of 2.3 million limestone blocks and took a workforce of 5,000 men more than 20 years to build.

TOMB ROBBERS KEEP OUT!

Anyone caught breaking into a royal tomb and trying to steal treasure will be impaled on a sharp stake and left to die a slow, painful death.

Enter at your own risk YOU HAVE BEEN WARNED!
By order of the pharaoh

WORKERS STRIKE!

Workmen building the royal tombs have put down their tools and are demanding better living conditions from the pharaoh. The men say they are hungry and thirsty. The official petition reads: **"We have no clothes, no fat, no fish and no vegetables."** Strike leaders claim the strike will continue until the workers' needs are met in full.

STEP INSIDE

The king's architect gives us an exclusive tour inside the Great Pyramid. "Sorry it's so dark, the rush torches don't shed much light. This passage slopes down inside the pyramid, then up to the king's burial chamber. We've built several empty chambers to confuse tomb robbers. Unfortunately, you may need to be executed now I've shown you the way!"

CAREERS GUIDE

VIZIER (chief minister)

This is the top civil service post — the pharaoh's right-hand man. Think mayor, top judge and chief tax collector rolled into one. Some viziers have even seized the throne from weak pharaohs. One drawback — the job is usually handed down from father to son, so you are very unlikely to land this key position.

Rating: ★★★★★
Definitely one to aim for

POTTER

Do you really want to spend all day scrabbling in a field with your clothes caked with mud? Or work at a rickety potter's wheel, with clay spraying everywhere? And the smoke from the furnace stings your eyes when you bake your pots…

Rating: ★ **One to avoid**

WEAVER

As a weaver you will slave all day in a gloomy, stuffy, weaving room, squatting with your knees drawn up to your chest. You have to bribe the doorkeeper with food to let you out into the daylight. If you dare to take a day off, it will be 50 lashes of the whip.

Rating: ★ **One for suckers**

SOLDIER

A great job if you fancy facing your mortal enemy armed with only a club or spear and wearing just an apron. If you get lucky and kill your enemy, do not forget to cut off his right hand so you can claim your reward in gold. In peacetime, you may have to work as a messenger or quarryman.

Rating: ★★★
Dangerous, but a good chance of booty

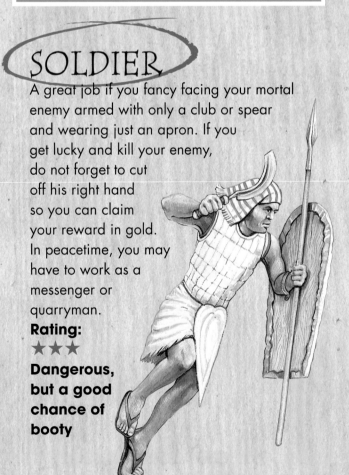

There is no shortage of work in ancient Egypt. Trouble is, most jobs are badly paid, dirty and back-breaking. Our careers expert Dua-Khety gives the lowdown on the best jobs to aim for — and the ones to avoid.

JOBS FOR THE GIRLS

Most women stay at home and look after the family, but you could be a weaver. If you are high born you can become a career wife and marry a top official. If you are well-educated you might try for priestess or even doctor. Party-lovers can become musicians, dancers or acrobats. Gloomy souls may apply for posts as official mourners.

SCRIBE

Now here's a job I thoroughly recommend. You will be your own boss, you will be well paid and you do not have to pay taxes. You keep records and write letters for everyone who cannot read, from the pharaoh down. A scribe qualification could land you a career as a doctor, priest or architect. The only drawback is you have to study for five years, between the ages of 9 and 14, when most kids are playing.

Rating: ★★★★

BRICKLAYER

Avoid like the plague unless you want to end each day utterly worn out. You will spend hours kneading animal dung to bake bricks – then eat without washing your hands. Lifting heavy bricks makes your kidneys ache.

Rating: A job for mugs only

OTHER JOBS TO AVOID

Washerman: Spend all day thigh-deep in the river bashing dirty clothes against a stone.

Messenger: See the world, but watch out for lions and bandits.

Thief: Very heavy penalties for tomb robbers (see page 11).

Fisherman: Beware perils including hippos, crocodiles and biting flies.

What's in Your FRIDGE?

Egyptians love to eat. At banquets, we have even been known to eat so much that we make ourselves sick! Royal good-time girl Cleopatra explains how to throw the banquet to end all banquets.

TEETH TROUBLE

by Hesire, our dental expert

We all — even the pharaohs — suffer from bad teeth. The bread contains grit and gives us cavities. Our fondness for sweet foods such as honey and dates causes tooth decay.

ON THE MENU

Bread made from wheat is the staple diet of Egypt. Beef is the nation's favourite meat, but lamb, goat, poultry, fish and the odd antelope steak also provide protein. Five-a-day fruit and veggies? Sure — choose from leeks, onions, garlic, cucumber, grapes, figs, dates and melons. The poor live on fish, beans and veggies seven days a week, but no one goes hungry.

BANQUET ETIQUETTE

CLEO SAYS:

⭐ At my banquets, celebrity guests eat while lying on a couch. Everyone else sits on the floor.

⭐ Food is served on low tables. Eat with your fingers.

⭐ A servant will bring water between courses, so there is really no need to wipe your hands on your clothes.

⭐ Beer and wine will flow freely. It is an insult to your hostess not to get drunk!

CLEO SAYS:

Smelling Sweetly

Perfume cones are a must at parties. All fashionable ladies wear cones of scented animal fat on their heads. As the party heats up, the fat melts and trickles down your wig. It's a bit messy, but the smell is fantastic!

PARTY ENTERTAINERS

★ ★ ★ ★ ★ ★ ★ ★ ★ ★ ★ ★

Look no further for that perfect party atmosphere. Let our dancing girls and acrobats entertain you. Female musicians perform on the harp, flute, tambourine, clappers and sacred rattle.

★ ★ ★ ★ ★ ★ ★ ★ ★

FOR HIRE

Reasonable Rates

Hell's Kitchen

Most food is cooked out of doors — it is far too hot inside to do a large spit-roast. In any case, as a good hostess you would not want smoke, fumes and spitting fat putting off your guests.

CLEO SAYS:

I've thrown hundreds of parties in my time. No expense is spared. We eat off gold plates and drink from jewelled cups. It has not been a good party unless my guests take several days to recover afterwards.

AVOID THE PONG

We do not have fridges in ancient Egypt, so to prevent food going bad, we salt our fish. Both fish and fowl are also dried in the sunshine. Otherwise our food would get stinky pretty quickly!

BANQUET MENU

Fancy breads

Calf's head
Whole roast ox
Spit-grilled goose and quail
Pigeon casserole
Baked fish
Vegetables in season

Sticky honey cakes
Figs, melons and pomegranates
Wine and beer

STYLE FILE

Style is all-important in Egyptian society. Everyone puts a lot of effort into looking good in public. Our style guru, Nefertiti, wife of our pharaoh Akhenaten, gives her tips on how to look your best.

CLOTHES SENSE

NEFERTITI SAYS:

"Don't bother trying to impress with a new look. Egyptian fashions have hardly changed in centuries. Men wear a kilt, women wear a simple shift dress or tunic, with a cloak if you're chilly. Pleated linen is all the rage at the moment. The main thing is to look clean and tidy, get your pleats straight and don't forget that dab of perfume!"

HOT ON HYGIENE

Tips on toilette by Nefertiti

Start to get ready for that glittering occasion by taking a shower. Get your servant to douse you in Nile water, preferably scented with lotus blossoms. Rub scented oil all over — lovely. Dress in your finest linen and do your makeup using your bronze mirror. Then just pop on your favourite wig, and you're ready to go!

Where's my wig?

Most Egyptians shave their heads to keep cool and avoid lice. Just pop on a wig before you appear in public. Rich people wear wigs made of real hair — sometimes with lice from the previous owner! There are super-curly wigs for special occasions. Poor people's wigs are made of wool, palm fibre or just plain grass.

MAD ABOUT MAKEUP

No self-respecting Egyptian man or woman would be seen dead or alive in public without a spot of makeup. We redden our lips and cheeks using ochre mixed with fat or water.

Green malachite

Everyone wears eye shadow made from green malachite, and eye liner — black kohl — made from charcoal. We sometimes use lead, but in fact it is poisonous, so do not try it at home!

Black kohl

GLAM IT UP!

Egyptians like their bling. Both men and women wear neck collars, rings, earrings and bangles — and the glitzier the better! Depending on your budget, your jewellery may be made of cheap glass beads or solid gold and precious jewels!

YOUTH STYLE

For boys and girls, the hot look is to have your head shaved except for one long, dangling lock of hair called the "sidelock of youth". Young people often wear very little — being naked is cool for kids and fine in public. After all, less is more!

PHARAOH OUTFITTERS

Kilts and dresses to suit every budget

✳ ✳ ✳ ✳

For the wealthy we have only the finest linen

✳ ✳ ✳ ✳

Our garments are so fine they're almost transparent!

✳ ✳ ✳ ✳

Coarser linen for the less wealthy

✳ ✳ ✳ ✳

Sandals in many sizes

For all your clothing needs!

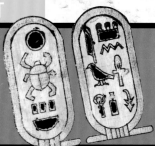

CELEBRITY

Our top deity, the Sun god Amun-Re, has shut the other gods and goddesses in the Great Temple at Karnak with teams of scribes recording their every move. The gods and goddesses explain why they should get to stay in the Big Brother temple and be voted the nation's favourite deity.

Did you know? Amun-Re is often shown with the head of a ram.

THOTH

Role: God of wisdom and learning
Appearance: Baboon or man with head of ibis bird
Thoth says:

"As god of knowledge, you'll need my help to pass exams. I also keep a little book in which I record every person's fate, so you'd be wise to vote for me."

KHEPRI

Role: God of rebirth
Appearance: Scarab beetle
Khepri says:

"I may look like a beetle rolling a ball of dung, but I'm one part of the Sun god. My dung is like the Sun rolling across the sky."

HATHOR

Role: Goddess of love, music, drinking and dancing
Appearance: Cow or woman with tall horns
Hathor says:

"Being shut up here is right up my street. Eat, drink and be merry!"

HORUS

Role: God of kingship and government, son of Isis and Osiris
Appearance: Hawk-headed man
Horus says:

"I'm patron to the pharaohs, and I have friends in high places. I can also cure snakebites, so I'm a handy guy."

BIG BROTHER

ISIS

Role: Goddess of wives and mothers, wife of Osiris, mother to Horus and protector to the abandoned Anubis

Appearance: Woman with a throne on her head

Isis says:

" I'm the ideal mother and wife and I'm pretty good at healing. And as goddess of women, I'm hoping to get the female vote. "

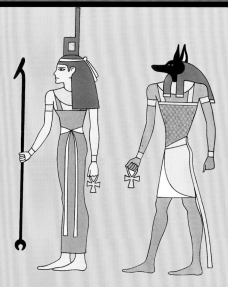

Isis with Anubis, god of mummification

OSIRIS

Role: God of the dead, husband of Isis, father of Horus

Appearance: Mummified pharaoh with green skin

Osiris says:

" I may not be pretty, but I'm lord of the Underworld, so it pays to keep on my good side. "

Did you know?

Seth, Osiris' brother, was jealous and killed Osiris, tearing his body into 14 pieces. Isis searched for the pieces and mended her husband.

KHNUM

Role: God of the Nile and also of pottery and potters

Appearance: Man with ram's head

Khnum says:

" I control the Nile's annual flood, which makes the land fertile. And I fashioned people from clay one day when I wasn't busy. "

MAKEOVER MUMMY

We Egyptians go to great efforts to preserve the bodies of our dead for the life hereafter. After an elaborate funeral, the corpse is buried with all the goods that the dead person will need in the afterlife. Our embalming expert, Anubis, explains how to make the ultimate mummy.

STEP-BY-STEP MUMMY

You will need:
- 1 dead body
- natron (preserving salt)
- 300 square metres (3,230 sq.ft) linen for bandages
- four canopic jars to store organs
- large pot of molten resin (tree sap)
- sawdust, ointment, flint knife and amulets

1. Wash the body and pack it in natron to preserve it.

2. Cut the body open using a flint knife. Remove the lungs, liver, stomach and intestines. Embalm and store in the canopic jars. Leave the heart — this will be needed for the gods to judge the spirit in the afterlife.

3. Use a long hook to pull the brain out through the nostrils. Discard this useless part of the body.

4. After 40 days, wash off the natron. Anoint the body with perfumed oil and use sawdust to stuff any limbs that look shrivelled.

5. Wrap the body in at least 20 layers of bandages, interspersed with amulets (lucky charms) to protect the corpse from evil spirits. Pop on a portrait mask. One mummy, ready for the coffin.

I MOURN YOUR LOSS

Professional mourner Mona Lot offers her services for that special funeral. Weeping, wailing and gnashing of teeth are all-inclusive. Extra for putting ash on my head and throwing myself on the ground.

AFTERLIFE.COM

GRAVE GOODS TO MEET ALL YOUR NEEDS IN THE AFTERLIFE

Simply click to choose from our wide range of:

These magical statues come to life to do your bidding in the next world.

Furnishings

Clothing

Weapons

Instruments

Foods

Shabti

ANUBIS EMBALMERS

We offer three ranges of embalming to suit every pocket

Economy range: The body is injected with cedar oil and packed in natron for 40 days.

Middle range: The organs are removed and preserved separately. The dried corpse is wrapped in bandages.

Luxury range: As the middle range, but wrapped in finest linen, with more than 20 amulets tucked into the bandages. Portrait masks made to order in plaster and resin or pure gold.

TREAT YOURSELF TO A RIGHT ROYAL FUNERAL

EMBALM-A-PET

We embalm your pet kitty, pooch or monkey to keep you company in the afterlife. Crocodiles? No problem, though we do charge extra. Our motto is if it moves, embalm it! However, we do advise clients that it is always best to wait until the animal is actually dead before starting the procedure.

WHAT A SEND-OFF!

Our pharaohs get a terrific send-off. After 70 days of embalming, the body is placed inside three coffins of increasing size, then a stone sarcophagus. The coffin is rowed across the river for the elaborate ceremony of Opening the Mouth, so the king's spirit can eat and drink in the afterlife. Prayers are offered, and food and drink are left daily at the tomb.

MEET THE
PHARAOHS

Egypt's pharaohs have incredible wealth and power. Unfortunately, all that power sometimes goes to their heads. *HAIL!* has all the latest gossip on our royal celebrities. Our court correspondent also has exclusive interviews with the high and mighty, printed in full.

LAP OF LUXURY

Congratulations to Old Kingdom pharaoh Pepi II, who has just celebrated his 100th birthday. Pepi came to the throne at the tender age of six and has now ruled for an amazing 94 years.

Q *What is the secret of your long life, your majesty?*

A My slaves do everything for me, so I've never had to lift a finger. I thoroughly recommend it. Can someone peel me a grape?

Pepi II as a child, sitting on his mother's knee.

SHORT AND SWEET?

1479 BC: *HAIL!* has breaking news that Tuthmosis III has at last taken over from his stepmother Hatshepsut, who has ruled as pharaoh for these past 22 years. Rumour has it that Tuthmosis has quite a chip on his shoulder. Not only is he just 1.5 metres (5 feet) tall, but he is really fed up with living in his stepmother's shadow. Tuthmosis says: "I may not be the world's tallest pharaoh, but I aim to be a big war hero." Looks like he plans to make up for lost time. Watch this space – and do not even think of calling him Shorty.

Did you know?

Pepi II's reign was the longest of any king in Egypt's history.

Beyond Belief

King Akhenaten is a pharaoh who dares to be different. He has banned all the old gods and set up his own religion, centred on the Sun god, Aten — a move that is unpopular.

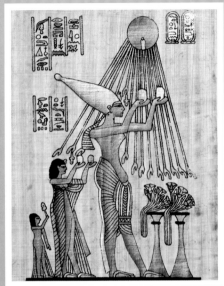

Q *So why did you reform Egypt's religion?*

A The country had more gods and goddesses than I've had hot dinners. The whole system needed streamlining. Then the Sun god appeared to me and I really saw the light.

Q *How has the new religion gone down with your people?*

A Not great, I admit, but give it time, they'll thank me one day.

Note: *They didn't, actually. The next king, Tutankhamun, restored the old religion, but that's another story — see pages 26–27.*

SOLDIER AND LOVER

Ramesses II is one of our mightiest ever pharaohs. He claims to have scored a great victory in his latest battle with the Hittites. Meanwhile, the great king has taken a new wife to add to his collection of eight royal wives and many lesser wives. He now has over 100 children!

Ramesses says: "A pharaoh's first duty is to produce a male heir. I just want to make sure that I have one."

SPHINX FACES

We like to remember our rulers. Sphinxes with human faces are sculpted after the pharaoh for whom they were built. The Great Sphinx at Giza (left) was built to honour King Kafre, whose pyramid is there. And there are six wonderful sphinxes of Queen Hatshepsut at her royal tomb at Deir el-Medina.

PROBLEM PAGE

Got a problem? Don't lose sleep over it. Share your troubles with *HAIL!*'s very own wise man, chief scribe Hesire. Hesire is a head doctor and dentist, so he can also help with your health problems.

Dear Wise Man
My current campaign against the Hittites is going badly. They made mincemeat of my army at the Battle of Kadesh. Should I come clean with my subjects, or try to cover it up?

Ramesses II

Dear Ramesses II
I'd say silence is golden. Just inscribe your new temple with pictures of your glorious victory at Kadesh and no one will know any different.

Hesire

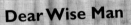

Dear Wise Man
I'm of royal blood, with plenty of experience of ruling with my husband, Tuthmosis II. Now the king has died, I'd like to take over, especially as my dear little stepson, Tuthmosis III, is far too young to rule. Only trouble is I'm female, and Egyptian rulers are always male. Any ideas?

Hatshepsut

Dear Hatshepsut
Dress in the king's robes and wear the pharaoh's ceremonial beard and you should be fine. Why not launch an expedition to a distant land and bring back fabulous treasure — that should distract attention.

Hesire

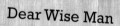

Dear Wise Man

My stepmother Hatshepsut has been ruling my kingdom for 21 years. She took over when I was a kid, but now I'm grown up, and she just won't do the decent thing and step down.

Tuthmosis III

Dear Tuthmosis

If the queen won't give up gracefully you may have to take matters into your own hands. Good luck with whatever you decide to do.

Hesire

Note: *HAIL! is sad to report that Queen Hatshepsut met a sudden, mysterious end soon after this letter was published. Long live the king!*

Dear Hesire

I became lovers with Roman general Julius Caesar to chum up to Rome and keep the throne of Egypt. But now a bunch of senators have gone and murdered him. Three consuls have taken power in Rome. What should I do?

Love and kisses, Cleopatra

Dear Hesire

Me again. Now that mad Hebrew slave, Moses, is hassling me to free his people. He is threatening all sorts of horrible plagues if I refuse. What should I do?

Ramesses II

Dear Ramesses

That's a tough one. If you let the Hebrews go, all the slaves will be wanting their freedom. On the other hand, I hear Moses has friends in high places. They say he can part the Red Sea with his wooden staff. You might be wise to give in, just this once.

Hesire

Dear Cleo

No use crying over spilt milk — or blood in this case. I'd advise making a play for one of the three consuls. They say Mark Antony is one for the ladies. It's worth a go.

Hesire

Note: *HAIL! is pleased to report that Cleopatra and Mark Antony are now an item. Exclusive pictures of the celebrity wedding next week.*

BOY-KING

The minute Tutankhamun became pharaoh he changed his name from Tutankhaten and turned his back on his father's religion. Where did this rebellion come from? He has even been restoring all the old statues and inscriptions that had been damaged by agents of Akhenaten.

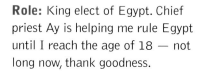

profile　　**Home　　Profile　　Inbox**

Tutankhamun

Wall

Role: King elect of Egypt. Chief priest Ay is helping me rule Egypt until I reach the age of 18 — not long now, thank goodness.

Favourite animals: My pet monkeys, giraffe and lion.

Interests: Hunting and playing senet (a game like chess).

Favourite people: My mum Kiya and my grandmother Tiye. Dad was OK too, but he did have wacky ideas.

Unfavourite people: Chief priest Ay is always trying to control me. The top general, Horemheb, also thinks he can boss me around.

Marital status: I recently married my half-sister Ankhesenamun.

Last updated: 1327 BCE

View Photos of Me (349)

My Profile

Photos

My last hunting trip

Tutankhamun became pharaoh in 1336 BCE when he was only nine years old. He was the son of Akhenaten, but broke with his father and restored the old religion. Was that his own idea, or did someone lean on him? *HAIL!* has the inside story, thanks to a scoop — access to the boy-king's blog!

TUT'S BLOG

Extracts from the boy-king's blog, beginning in 1338BCE, two years before he became pharaoh:

1338 BCE Dad is really shaking things up! Last year he transformed Egypt's religion. That annoyed a lot of people, especially the chief priest, Ay. Now he's built a new capital at El Amarna. We've just moved here from Thebes. The palace is pretty cool — modern art everywhere.

1336 BCE Dad died suddenly last week. It's really sad, but at least I get to be pharaoh! How cool is that! Chief priest Ay and General Horemheb say they're going to help steer the kingdom until I'm old enough to take control.

1333 BCE Being pharaoh isn't all it's cracked up to be. Ay is making me marry my half-sister Ankhesenamun. She's OK, but more like a friend — we grew up together. Now Ay says we've got to move back to Thebes.

1328 BCE Ay is seriously annoying me. He's made me restore the old religion and now he's pulling down all the temples that Dad built. Thank goodness I'm 18 next year and take full control. My first act will be to send Ay packing!

POLICE REPORT

Filed by Sergeant Smenkhkare 1327 BCE:

I was summoned to the palace in the early hours. Chief priest Ay said that the young king had met with a tragic accident. I arrived to find the boy-king lying unconscious with a severe injury to his leg. Ay said he had suffered a 'hunting accident'. We suspect foul play, and palace staff are obviously frightened, but there is no way of proving it either way.

BOY-KING MEETS SUDDEN END

HAIL! is sad to report that young prince Tutankhamun has died suddenly after a hunting accident. Ironically, the young king was due to assume full power next week. Rumours that the boy-pharaoh was murdered have been quashed by chief priest Ay, who now takes the throne. Tutankhamun's funeral will take place 70 days from now in a secret location. Shame, the boy-king seemed like such a nice young man.

Online CATALOGUE

Egyptians are big spenders. Our ships ply the River Nile, Mediterranean Sea and Red Sea, carrying luxuries from every corner of the known world. Our online catalogue will take care of all your shopping needs with the click of a button. Food, jewellery, furniture, clothes, weapons, live animals and tools — you shop, we drop!

BUY OR BARTER

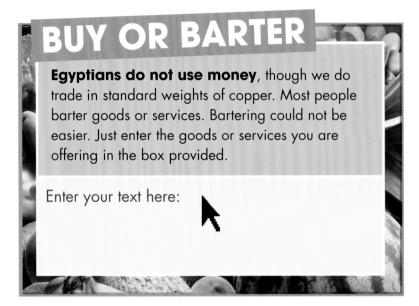

Egyptians do not use money, though we do trade in standard weights of copper. Most people barter goods or services. Bartering could not be easier. Just enter the goods or services you are offering in the box provided.

Enter your text here:

EXOTIC PETS ONLINE

By appointment to the pharaoh
BABOONS, LIONS, LEOPARDS and GIRAFFES
in stock to add to your private zoo
No palace is complete without our magnificent animals

We guarantee no mange or rabies

INCENSE FROM THE LAND OF PUNT

EXCLUSIVE OFFER!

Queen Hatshepsut's expedition has come back from the Land of Punt with myrrh and frankincense to burn in the temples

Whole myrrh bushes
BOGOFF — Buy One Get One Free

WRITING MADE EASY

SCRIBE for HIRE!

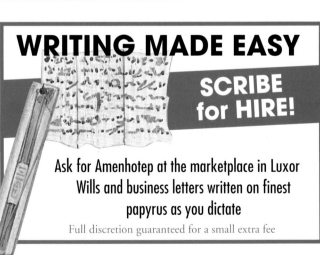

Ask for Amenhotep at the marketplace in Luxor
Wills and business letters written on finest papyrus as you dictate

Full discretion guaranteed for a small extra fee

Nubia, a Shoppers' Paradise

Our amazing kingdom south of Egypt supplies gold, spices, elephant tusks, panther skins and giraffe-tail whisks to all who can afford it.

Look no further for all your luxury goods

Get the best bargains here!

PYGMY WANTED

To: Harkhuf, Governor of Elephantine, Southern Egypt

Dear Mr Harkhuf

I hear you captured a pygmy who is a great dancer on your recent trip to southern Africa. Brilliant! My dad, Pepi I, says we definitely want him at the palace, and I am desperate to see him. Please take extra care of him on the boat journey. Check him ten times a night and make sure he does not fall overboard.

Yrs, Pepi II aged 9
PS Dad says damaged goods will not be acceptable.

GRAND WEAPONS SALE

Booty from our latest skirmish with the Hittites
Second-hand spears, bows, swords, shields and armour
Quality workmanship by Asian craftsmen

We wipe the blood off first!!

FRESHEN UP YOUR TOMB

Is your family tomb looking dull and dowdy? A lick of paint will make it as good as new
Just leave it to our expert decorators
No job too large or small

TOP QUALITY GUARANTEED

NILE SHIPPERS

FOR ALL YOUR TRANSPORT NEEDS
We ship bulk goods — minerals, grain, cedarwood from Lebanon, stone blocks for pyramid building, etc.

Half your money back if delivery is late

GLOSSARY

afterlife The life after death; to the ancient Egyptians, death was a rebirth into the afterlife.

architect Someone who designs and supervises the construction of buildings and other large structures.

barter To swap or bargain, trading goods without the exchange of money.

canopic jar A jar used to preserve certain body organs, put there during mummification.

consul An official appointed by the government of one country to represent its interests and the welfare of its citizens in another country.

embalm To treat a body with chemicals in order to preserve it.

hieroglyphics The ancient Egyptian script, a form of picture writing.

Hittites An ancient people who established an empire that covered most of modern Turkey and Syria.

kohl A powder used as a cosmetic to darken the eyelids, eyebrows, etc.

mastaba An ancient Egyptian rectangular tomb made of bricks.

mummification To embalm and dry a body in order to preserve it.

mummy Describes the dead body of a person embalmed and preserved for burial.

natron A type of salt used in mummification.

necropolis The burial ground, or cemetery, of an ancient city.

ochre An earthy mixture of minerals that are used as pigments for colouring.

papyrus A water reed used to make paper, rope and many other objects.

pharaoh The title given to Egyptian kings.

plague An epidemic disease that causes many deaths.

Ptolemies The kings of the Macedonian dynasty that ruled Egypt 323–30 BC.

sarcophagus A stone coffin.

scribe An educated man in ancient Egypt who could read and write and worked as a clerk.

shabti A small statue placed in the tomb to work as a servant in the afterlife.

silt Sediment deposited by flowing water.

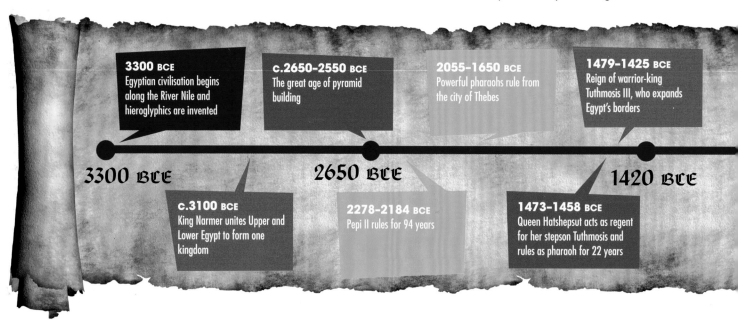

3300 BCE
Egyptian civilisation begins along the River Nile and hieroglyphics are invented

c.2650–2550 BCE
The great age of pyramid building

2055–1650 BCE
Powerful pharaohs rule from the city of Thebes

1479–1425 BCE
Reign of warrior-king Tuthmosis III, who expands Egypt's borders

3300 BCE   2650 BCE   1420 BCE

c.3100 BCE
King Narmer unites Upper and Lower Egypt to form one kingdom

2278–2184 BCE
Pepi II rules for 94 years

1473–1458 BCE
Queen Hatshepsut acts as regent for her stepson Tuthmosis and rules as pharaoh for 22 years

www.bbc.co.uk/history/ancient/egyptians Plenty of subjects to explore including pyramids, mummification, gods and beliefs, pharaohs and daily life in ancient Egpyt.

www.egyptologyonline.com/mummification.htm Everything there is to know about the process of mummification.

www.carnegiemnh.org/exhibitions/egypt/ The Carnegie Museum of Natural History site about life in ancient Egypt.

www.nationalgeographic.com/pyramids/pyramids.html Explore the secrets of the pyramids of ancient Egypt on this site with timelines and facts about the builders and building.

www.ancientegypt.co.uk/ The British Museum, London, site has information about life in ancient Egypt, its geography, gods and goddesses, mummification, the pharaohs, pyramids, trades and writing.

www.guardians.net/egypt/kids/index.htm Fascinating facts about ancient

Egypt and its peoples, with links to games, crafts and quizzes.

www.historyforkids.org/learn/egypt A comprehensive site about every aspect of life in ancient Egypt, including religion, clothing, food, writing and architecture.

BOOKS

Step Into...Ancient Egypt
by Philip Steele (Southwater, 2008)

If I Were a Kid in Ancient Egypt
by Cobblestone Publishing (Cricket Books, 2007)

Eyewitness Books; Ancient Egypt
by George Hart (Dorling Kindersley, 2008)

Explore Within an Egyptian Mummy
by Lorraine Jean Hopping (Silver Dolphin Books, 2008)

The Gruesome Truth About the Egyptians by Jillian Powell (Wayland, 2010)

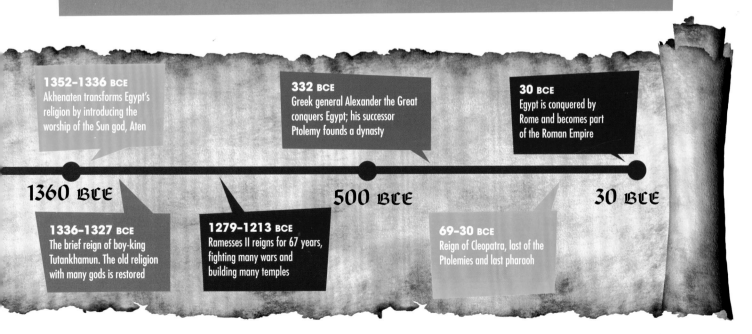

1352–1336 BCE
Akhenaten transforms Egypt's religion by introducing the worship of the Sun god, Aten

332 BCE
Greek general Alexander the Great conquers Egypt; his successor Ptolemy founds a dynasty

30 BCE
Egypt is conquered by Rome and becomes part of the Roman Empire

1360 BCE

500 BCE

30 BCE

1336–1327 BCE
The brief reign of boy-king Tutankhamun. The old religion with many gods is restored

1279–1213 BCE
Ramesses II reigns for 67 years, fighting many wars and building many temples

69–30 BCE
Reign of Cleopatra, last of the Ptolemies and last pharaoh

INDEX